QUESTIONS

FOR

TERRIBLE
PEOPLE

250 QUESTIONS  **TO ANSWER**

D1628172

WES HAZARD

Adams Media

New York   London   Toronto   Sydney   New Delhi

Adams Media
An Imprint of Simon & Schuster, Inc.
57 Littlefield Street
Avon, Massachusetts 02322

For information about special discounts for bulk purchases, please contact Simon & Schuster Special Sales at 1-866-506-1949 or business@simonandschuster.com.

The Simon & Schuster Speakers Bureau can bring authors to your live event. For more information or to book an event contact the Simon & Schuster Speakers Bureau at 1-866-248-3049 or visit our website at www.simonspeakers.com.

Manufactured in the United States of America

10 9 8 7 6 5 4

Library of Congress Cataloging-in-Publication Data has been applied for.

ISBN 978-1-4405-9752-7
ISBN 978-1-4405-9753-4 (ebook)

ACKNOWLEDGMENTS

I'd like to thank my mom for always being there, my best friend Dave for enduring endless text message exchanges about the relative morality of grave-robbing vs. allowing every panda on the planet to perish, and my graduate degree in poetry writing for giving me the necessary sense of the ridiculous for this project. Finally, my editor Eileen has my eternal gratitude for making this delightful insanity possible.

INTRODUCTION

Perhaps it all started when I got an e-mail from my food delivery service informing me that my pizza order was canceled because the driver was in an accident. Instead of feeling bad for the guy, my first reaction was to think, "Damn, I guess it's a steak and cheese sub again." Or maybe it was during a recent 30-minute odyssey to find a parking spot when I started fantasizing about which physical impairment I'd agree to in order to get a handicapped parking pass. In any case, regardless of the exact moment it dawned on me, I've come to realize that I can be a less than stellar person on the regular. Terrible even.

After talking to some good friends (and wading through the comments section on any given viral web article) I realized that I'm not alone. Maybe, just maybe, there are some literal saints among us. But for the most part, we've all had our share of whispered insults, elaborate revenge fantasies, hypothetical devil's bargains, and twisted thought experiments about what awful thing we'd do to get out of the awful situation we presently find ourselves in. And it's okay.

That's why this book was written. To help you find out what you, your friends, your family, or that person you just met at a party would do when the choices get weird and a person's true character is revealed. Some of these questions are just for laughs and others might make you reconsider ever turning your back on your best friend again. Either way, you should learn a lot about yourself and those close to you. So go on. Sit down with some people who feel like being honest and see where it takes you.

From there I think the best we can do is appreciate everyone for their own particular brand of terrible, laugh at it when possible, and try—at least try—to help each other be better. Remember: Whenever someone throws a bunch of negativity at you, especially a total stranger, they just might be in the middle of the worst day of their life. That's probably not the case, but it might be, and you should keep that in mind before throwing it right back at them.

QUESTIONS

Offer: You'll get $20 million to spend however you wish, but in exchange you must collect and store every drop of your own urine for the rest of your life. Do you accept?

You can have any large animal (either living or extinct) shrunk down to pug size and given to you as a pet. You have to keep it for at least a year. What's your choice?

Keep in mind that a cuddly grizzly bear is still going to need a few pounds of fresh meat per week, and how cool is your landlord really?

Take out your phone.
Fuck, Marry, Kill the last three people you texted with.

Bonus points: Text them your decision.

You're in a public park on a sunny afternoon. You have 15 minutes to either make a random child cry or provoke a grown man to punch you in the face. Which do you choose? (Follow up: How do you do it?)

There's significant opportunity for a two-for-one here . . .

You're in the bathroom of a crowded, filthy dive bar after just having lost a non-negotiable bet to your best friend. Would you rather lick the toilet seat or walk out of the bathroom naked?

Pick your preferred erogenous zone: Would you rather have a penis the size of a soda can or the size of a roll of Life Savers? Would you rather have breasts the size of basketballs or marbles?

Would you rather lose your cellphone or have your pet hamster die?

I mean, I loved my hamster as a kid. But let's be honest, he never knew the names and numbers of all my friends and family, and he definitely couldn't work a camera worth a damn . . .

You've been given the power to instantly cure everyone in the world who has herpes and also eradicate the disease from the face of the earth, but to do so, you personally have to abstain from sex for the rest of your life. Do you do it?

Just think of how often you'd get laid for being such a selfless and altruistic hero for millions! Oh, wait . . .

Your best friend is being held hostage by a crazed sports fan. The maniac will release your friend unharmed, but in exchange you have to either take a full-force tackle from an NFL linebacker (you are not wearing pads, but he is) or jump out of a second-story window. You have 30 seconds to decide. Go!

They'll both hurt a lot, but which one is going to give you the better dinner party story? Think about it . . .

During a morning walk, you find a freshly dead body on the side of a secluded road. Before you panic, you notice that a few folded $100 bills are clearly sticking out of the corpse's shirt pocket. Think carefully: Do you take the money?

Bonus: Do you report the body to the authorities?

Either you complete a full regimen of sex reassignment therapy and surgery (you don't have to pay for it) or one of your best friends will die suddenly and violently within a year. No one but you will ever know which you choose. What do you do?

If you and your parents had gone to the same high school at the same time, would you have talked to each other? Would you have been friends? Would you have been enemies?

You're producing an adult film. For your lead actors, you have to cast your choice of any U.S. president alongside any superhero. Who do you pick for each? What's the movie called?

Some actual presidential and superhero names and nicknames: Warren G. Harding, Tricky Dick Nixon, Whizzer, Shocker, and Uncle Jumbo. Seriously, Grover Cleveland was known as both Uncle Jumbo and Big Steve.

You randomly find the diary of the person you've been crushing on for years. In it they reveal their fears, desires, strongest memories, and ambitions. Do you read the whole thing and use the deeply personal information to woo them? Bonus: If you get them, would you ever tell them what you've done?

Pro tip: Never tell!

You're tasked with either digging up a grave and spending the night next to the coffin by yourself or killing a dog. If you refuse to do either, a random coworker will die suddenly. Do you complete one of the tasks? Which?

No one ever wants to hurt a dog, but remember:
Graves are like really, really deep.

Think about how often you currently watch NASCAR, if at all. Now imagine that it was 100 percent guaranteed that, if you watched, each race would feature a giant, multicar, fiery explosion (which may or may not involve flaming debris flying into the trackside audience). Would you watch more NASCAR?

You've been given the ability to watch and then publicly leak (anonymously) the sex tape of anyone you know personally. The person you choose will be identified in the video and will have to deal with the full consequences of your actions, as well as all the Internet and media attention. Who do you pick?

Don't forget: You can always choose yourself.

There's no way around it. Your best friend is going to be executed. You cannot save them. You are, however, granted the ability to choose whether they will be drowned, burned alive, placed in a gas chamber, or strapped to an electric chair. You cannot consult with them on their preference. Which do you choose?

Would you rather watch a feature-length hardcore porn film with your parents or watch a feature-length hardcore porn film starring your parents?

Either way, Thanksgiving (or direct eye contact with mom and dad) will probably never be quite the same.

What is one embarrassing fact about you that you're certain no one else on the planet knows?

Someone has a gun to your head. You've got exactly 1 minute to think of something (a text, video, photo, anything) to post on Facebook. If your post gets fewer than 100 likes in 1 hour, you'll be killed. The post cannot reveal the situation or directly plead for likes in any way. What do you post?

Some reliable standby possibilities include: A heartfelt confession and apology for a secret past transgression, an announcement that you're finally ready to come out of the closet (even if you're not currently in it), or a 70-year-old photograph of a grandparent and a story about how awesome they were.

Would you rather go streaking on the playing field during a nationally televised sporting event or through a small suburban elementary school's playground during recess? Keep in mind that real world consequences apply if you are caught or identified.

Now's a good time to lace up those Nikes.

You need to get arrested within the next hour, but you need to be out (at least on bail) by tomorrow morning. If you fail at either, you'll lose a limb. What's your plan?

Here's hoping you paid attention during all those episodes of *Law & Order* you binge-watched . . .

Tomorrow morning, your spouse will wake up having forever lost the ability to see one of the major colors.* Anything of that color will appear as gray to them. You have the ability to choose which color goes. What's your choice?

*And by major I mean one of the colors you'd find in a Crayola 8-pack. You can't pick goldenrod or teal or some bullshit color like that.

Pop quiz: Would you rather be beaten to death with: a) a lead pipe, b) an Academy Award statue or, c) a bowling pin? Explain your reasoning in detail.

Just be thankful it's not an American Music Award. That would just be shameful.

What is the most nonsexual thought you've ever had during sex?

Making a podcast playlist in your head while getting it on doesn't make you a terrible person. It makes you a boring person . . .

For the rest of your life, prizefight entrance music will play each time you're about to masturbate. What's your song and why?

You can't pick the *Rocky* theme. You're better than that.

You've just taken over the Tooth Fairy's position and you need to cut costs. Instead of cash, what will you now be placing under children's pillows?

Let's think about the simple economic fact that lost teeth are by far your most abundantly held asset. Can you pay for a soda with a handful of molars?

Would you rather have the ability to fly, but only at walking speed and with a max height of 10 feet above the ground, or be given the ability to biologically generate a superfast Wi-Fi network at will?

Crystal-clear Netflix every hour of the day or realizing your dream of becoming a birthday balloon? Decisions, decisions . . .

Which would you rather wear every day for the rest of your life: Crocs shoes or thong underwear?

No one needs to know you're wearing thong underwear. Once I see that you wear Crocs (and aren't a nurse or restaurant server), that's the only thing I know about you.

If BuzzFeed wrote a list article about your life, what would be three things on your list of the "15 Reasons People Think You're an Awful Person"?

If your entire life was being recorded and broadcast on TV, as in the film *The Truman Show*, which network would you find yourself on and why?

Remember, you're not any less valuable as a person if it's not a for-profit channel. PBS has had consistently amazing programming for decades.

You're at Thanksgiving dinner with your whole family. You have to ruin the holiday with one sentence said out loud to everyone. What do you say or do?

It's a great way to let your fiancé know if you have a flip-the-table-over-and-scream-at-each-other type of family, or a sit-in-strained-silence-while-a-lone-family-member-cries-in-the-next-room type of family.

Take out your phone. You have 10 seconds to send a mass text containing one of your ten most recent photos to all of your contacts. You cannot explain or provide any context at all. Which image do you send?

You are forced to choose one person in your life to live out a single episode of any television show as whichever character you'd prefer for the rest of eternity on repeat. Which person, show, and character do you choose?

Think about it, you can be generous: Stefan Urquelle from *Family Matters*, Don Draper from *Mad Men*, Olivia Pope from *Scandal*. Or you can be harsh: Barney from *The Simpsons*, Oscar the Grouch from *Sesame Street*. But there's no need to keep it fictional. Snooki from *Jersey Shore* and Ozzy Osbourne from *The Osbournes* count.

Pee-wee Herman, Gilbert Gottfried, Fran Drescher, Sarah Palin, or Ray Romano. Which of these people would you choose to narrate every moment of your waking life, Discovery Channel–style, for a full month?

You and your coworkers are trapped for a year at your workplace with no exit and no food. How long until you resort to cannibalism to survive and who's getting eaten first?

If the HR rep offered an incentive program that included 2 years of paid vacation for each limb you voluntarily give up, would you be on board? I mean . . . do you really need two arms?

You receive an unsolicited nude photo from a cellphone number you don't recognize. It was clearly meant for someone else, but you like what you see. Do you respond? If not, do you delete it forever and never say a word or do you keep it?

You have a vocally religious coworker who happens to consistently make dismissive and critical comments about homosexuality. One day you find a screenshot of their profile page from a gay-kink meet-up site being shared on an online forum. Do you take any action, and if so, what?

Think of the person in your life that you like the least. You're going to lock them in a dark basement for an entire night and play a single song on repeat at high volume. What track do you pick?

Who remembers all the words to "Mambo No. 5" by Lou Bega?

Would you rather find yourself suddenly having to: a) deliver a random baby, b) pull off an emergency plane landing (you'd be coached through it from the airport control tower), or c) hold a stranger's hand as they pass away after an accident?

Landing the plane successfully is definitely going to get you the greatest and most widespread accolades. Then again, messing it up would likely just kill you.

Would you rather be dirt poor and thought of as a total saint by your friends, family, and community or be filthy rich and regarded as a total scumbag by everyone you meet?

Remember, money can't buy you love, but you can definitely pay people to pretend to like you.

You get to be the Judeo-Christian God for 5 minutes, just enough time to slip an eleventh commandment into the Scripture. It can be anything you want. What is your choice?

The Grim Reaper has thrown down the gauntlet and challenged you to a friendly competition. If you win, you get 10 extra years of a healthy and energetic life. If you lose, you die today. You get to choose the activity (it can be anything: Chess, cornhole, a dance-off). What do you pick and why?

You arrive home to find your apartment complex is on fire. You rush into the blaze and find that you will only be able to save either your pet gerbil, whom you love very much, or your neighbor's 92-year-old aunt who's always been kind of mean to you. You only have time for one. What do you do?

Like the saying goes, what happens in the burning building stays in the burning building . . .

Would you rather attend a funeral while high on laughing gas or go to your own wedding doped up on horse tranquilizers?

Just remember: A professional photographer is usually only present at *one* of these occasions.

You get instantly transported to Neanderthal times with only the knowledge in your head and whatever you have in your pockets or purse right now. What do you do to establish dominance and avoid being beaten to death by a caveman?

Which movie villain would you be willing to date in real life (for at least a year)?

And no cheating. I'm talking villain, not antihero. You don't get any points for grabbing coffee with Robert De Niro from *Taxi Driver*.

The world is ending in 5 minutes. You have time to make one phone call. Do you call a loved one that you've already expressed your love for many times over the course of your lifetime, or do you call up the person you've secretly despised for years and curse them out like you've always dreamed of?

Give this some thought. Mom *definitely* knows you love her. Carl from Accounting probably thinks he's on your good side. Just saying . . .

You have 60 seconds of total access to the e-mail and social media accounts of the person you like the least in the world. What damage are you going to do? (Keep in mind that no one will ever know it was you!)

You really should think about this right now and have the answer ready because when the time comes you're only going to get one chance.

You're a comic book villain. Without making any reference to your powers, backstory, or goals, what would your arch-nemesis superhero be like? Describe in detail.

You get to play zoological mad scientist and swap the behavior and temperament of one animal with the body of another. You'll keep one of the resulting creatures as a pet and unleash the other to wreak havoc on your neighborhood. What animals do you switch and why?

I'm strongly leaning toward a sloth with the attitude of a honey badger. Sure, it won't be able to do very much damage at all, but I think the idea of being "chased" by something that wants to tear you apart but can only move at 2 meters per second has a certain nightmare quality about it.

You've been tasked with writing Genghis Khan's college admission essay. You have to be honest, but you also have to actually be persuasive. What are three "qualities" you'd choose to focus on and how would you spin them?

You can do it . . . somehow. Just remember Ted Bundy got into college . . . twice.

You either cut off your own pinky toe (your choice on which foot) or your best friend will wake up tomorrow having lost their right eye. Which do you choose?

Would you rather be peed on by 10 strangers simultaneously or drink a cup of your own urine?

In either case you could almost certainly make some pretty sweet coin if you decided to release a video of it . . .

If all of your exes gathered in a room, what would they agree on as the weirdest or most annoying thing you do in bed?

If you get more than three separate answers, maybe re-evaluate your approach.

Your best friend must
go to prison. Without
consulting them, you
must choose whether
they spend 1 year in
solitary confinement
(access to books but
no mail, phone calls,
or human interaction)
or if they get 5 years in
general population with
regular visits from friends
and family. What do you
choose for them?

Your mom walks in on you masturbating or you must watch a video of your own conception. Which do you choose?

You enter a public restroom stall and see that not only was the toilet well used by the previous occupant, but it has not been flushed. You also see some cash floating under and among the foulness. How much money would you have to see to start grabbing bills?

Money can buy many things, but it cannot flush away memories . . .

You've designed a dating app with a naughty one-word title. What's it called and what's the hook?

You have the power to
wipe tuberculosis off
the face of the earth
so that no one will
ever die from it again,
but in order to do so,
you have to become
paralyzed from the
waist down for the
rest of your life. No
one would ever know
of your sacrifice. Do
you do it?

Fill in the blanks: I promised _____ that I would never tell _____ about _____, and I never have.

. . . well . . . until now . . .

At what moment in your childhood would it have been the most dangerous to grant you omnipotence and a taste for banishing people into cornfields for the rest of their lives (like that crazy jack-in-the-box kid from *The Twilight Zone*)?

Jesus, the Buddha, and Mr. Rogers. Which one of these dudes would you most like to have as a roommate in a three-bedroom apartment?

Once he has signed the lease, the two of you will use Craigslist to fill the other spot.

If a big network started a reality show of live public executions of convicted criminals, who would be the best three-person celebrity hosting team?

It's certainly not required, but in this scenario one of the hosts can be the exhumed corpse of a celebrity. After all, Siskel was nothing without Ebert . . .

It's the year 500 B.c. in ancient Rome. You are the leader of a major army. If you could make any currently existing animal horse-sized, what animal would you choose to ride into battle to inspire fear in your enemies?

Hamsters have more potential than you think . . .

How many weeks of paid vacation would it take for you to commit to an Andy Dufresne sewage crawl like at the end of *The Shawshank Redemption*?

Note: You receive no extra sick time to deal with potential leprosy or PTSD.

Someone's taken your personal scent after playing soccer on a hot day and bottled it to be sold as cologne or perfume. What's the product called?

Who's the celebrity spokesperson?

What would be the three must-play tracks on your funeral playlist? At least one of them must be an embarrassing guilty pleasure.

I suggest getting this in writing somewhere immediately. You never know what could happen.

You get to send a fortune cookie–length message to yourself from 10 years ago. What do you say?

Bonus points for rhyming . . .

Be honest with yourself: What's the most that you could reasonably charge someone for sex with you?

Really get in there and assess your fair market value.

Name a situation where, looking back, you realize you were completely the villain?

It hurts, I know, but every once in a while you're going to have this moment of clarity.

How many lower-profile endangered species would you let perish in order to go back in time and relive one of the greatest moments of your life?

How much do we really *need* the Siamese crocodile?

What would be the title of the Lifetime network original movie made about you?

Choose wisely, because Lifetime has been kicking ass with their movies for decades now. You're going up against classics like *Cyber Seduction: His Secret Life*; *Mother, May I Sleep With Danger?*; and *Sexting in Suburbia*. Top those if you can . . .

Would you rather know the exact moment of your own death or be shown a video of exactly how it will happen?

Look at your last few days' worth of sent text messages; which single line do you choose to be engraved on your tombstone?

Anyone who gets buried with nothing more than "You up???" chiseled in granite to mark their final resting place will instantly become my personal hero, and I promise to leave a bouquet of roses at your grave once a year until I myself die.

You're in a good ol'-
fashioned slasher movie
being hunted down by a
crazed killer. Would you
rather be the first victim
who gets taken out quickly
and never sees it coming,
the best friend who's killed
right before the climax
of the movie, or the last
person standing whose
friends have all died
horrible deaths and who
now risks getting terrorized
in a sequel?

Would you rather eat a kitten or slap a random toddler in the face one time?

Would you agree to being made fabulously wealthy if, in exchange, each of your fingers would be transformed into a large writhing maggot for 1 hour each day?

It's gross, I know, but remember: Maggots are nature's "recyclers." Also, money.

Would you rather smell faintly of marijuana or strongly of Axe body spray for the rest of your life?

Either way, you're probably not going to have a lot of luck in job interviews.

Your life depends on you completely ruining your relationship with your best friend. You have 2 minutes alone with full access to their cellphone. What do you do?

The possibilities are really endless here! You can try sending a breakup text to their significant other or an "I quit" e-mail to their boss. Maybe change their voicemail message to a parody of a 1-800 sex line recording. Use your imagination!

Would you choose to become 50 percent more physically attractive in exchange for having your Internet limited to dial-up speed for the next 15 years?

Sure, you'd probably be able to get way more people to Netflix and chill with you, but good luck getting your Netflix to actually stream.

Your home is haunted. Would you prefer a ghost that silently watches you have sex or a ghost that whispers creepy riddles at you while you're going to the bathroom?

What question can never be answered with a "Yes"? Answer: "Are you dead?" Mwhahaha!

How much money would it take for you to do porn once, under an alias, in an unremarkable, low-budget production that your friends and family will (probably) never see?

Remember, the Internet is a vast ocean of secrets.

Tell the truth: Would you allow pandas to go extinct if it meant you had to abstain from booze, drugs, and caffeine for the rest of your life? (No one would ever know that all the pandas are gone because of you.)

Would you rather go colorblind or have every character in every dream you have for the rest of your life look and talk like Donald Trump?

The one small saving grace here is that you can't see the color orange.

Would you rather have all of your body hair replaced with pubic hair or be 100 pounds heavier for the rest of your life?

Would you rather do 10 years of hard time in a tough prison and be given $50 million on your release or be dirt poor for the rest of your life, but remain free?

Which would you rather have go viral: An Instagram account consisting solely of pictures of you on the toilet or a Gawker article with word-for-word excerpts from the diary you kept when you were thirteen?

Would you agree to have your genitals smell like rancid garlic for 5 years in exchange for saving dolphins from extinction?

Dolphins are considered one of the smartest animals on earth. What kind of monster are you?

Would you rather have a spouse who can only communicate in Insane Clown Posse lyrics while in bed or one whose reflection in any mirror looks exactly like Larry the Cable Guy?

Yes, you still have to touch them. No, you can't get a divorce.

If you were given the opportunity to be in the audience at Ford's Theatre on the night of Abe Lincoln's fateful visit, would you stop the assassination if it meant that you would be convicted and hanged for attempted murder and John Wilkes Booth and accomplices go free, or would you let the assassination happen?

Make a choice: Either you can't bathe for 2 years or every sex partner you have for the rest of your life cannot have bathed for 10 days prior to your romantic evening.

Either option presents some intriguing possibilities for a potential future as a Febreze spokesperson.

Who would you rather sit next to on a 12-hour flight: Michael Vick or Jared the Subway Guy? Which would you rather get high with?

Take out your phone. Rank the last ten people you've texted in order from who you'd like to bang most to who you'd dread banging the most.

Bonus points: Shoot #1 a text. You never know what could happen.

Would you rather your first-born child had the eyes of Steve Buscemi or the personality of Kanye West?

I'm just going to state right now that no, abandoning your child in a forest is not an option here.

Who would you rather complete an online dating profile for you: Your most recent ex or your father?

Just think of the top-shelf dad jokes you could score. How do you make a Kleenex dance? Put a little boogie in it . . .

Would you accept $3 million in cash in exchange for being listed as a level-one offender on your local sex offender registry? (You haven't actually harmed anyone and have not been incarcerated at all.)

Things to keep in mind: Future employment prospects, international travel, the fact that those records are publicly available online, vigilante justice, and the shamed look on your mother's face.

If everyone in the world had your values and priorities, what would be the main cause of World War III?

In my universe, 270 million people died because someone failed to move out of the way at the bottom of an escalator. Sigh . . .

You're standing on the bank of a swift-moving river when your pet dog of 6 years falls in. At the exact same time an elderly man you've never seen before also falls in. You are equidistant from your dog and the dude. You can save one. Who do you swim to?

You're spying on your neighbor through binoculars as they undress (creeper). All of a sudden their spouse bursts in, murders them, and then flees. When the police are called, it turns out the spouse has a strong alibi and is not considered a suspect. Do you inform the police of what you've seen if it meant everyone would know you are a perverted Peeping Tom?

Like, very public knowledge. The case is huge in the news and your voyeurism becomes a late-night talk show monologue staple.

Think of any gruesome crime that comes to mind. What summer blockbuster movie tagline can you come up with that would make people want to see it if they didn't know what it actually was about?

Remember: The Hollywood marketing machine made *Speed Racer* look pretty damn good before it came out. You can do this!

What mainstream Hollywood actor would you want to play you in the porn movie adaptation of your life?

What one sentence could you say to a 6-year-old that would shatter them for life?

They already know Santa Claus doesn't exist.

You are given $5 million. The catch is you aren't allowed to spend any of it on yourself. Instead you can only use the money to annoy, harass, belittle, and otherwise make life difficult for people you don't like (either people you know or public figures). You can't break the law or physically harm them. What do you do?

If you were a ghost haunting a modern couple in a typical apartment, what's the creepiest thing you could do to scare them shitless?

Assume that you have all the standard ghostly powers plus access to all of their devices and social media accounts.

Would you endure a 3-week hangover in order to spare a stranger from being murdered?

What's the meanest gift you could purchase for one of your family members, but still pass it off as well intentioned?

No one can hurt you like your family. Use this truth wisely . . .

Which two characters from film, television, or literature would you like to see engage in a gladiator-style baseball bat fight in a packed arena with all ticket sales going to charity?

Personally, I would go so far as to make T-shirts for Jar Jar Binks from the *Star Wars* prequels vs. Tom Bombadil from the *Lord of the Rings* novels.

You and your best friend are applying for the same job that you both really want. You are equally qualified, but this is your friend's only employment prospect while you have multiple promising interviews lined up. You're tight with the job recruiter, who has just told you the trick question every candidate gets asked. Do you share the information with your friend?

Just remind your friend that being a gainfully employed member of society isn't everything.

You're sitting alone at a café. At the table next to you, two strangers are having an obvious first date that seems to be going really well. When one of them goes to the restroom, the other (who you're really attracted to) starts chatting you up and asks if they could have your number. Do you give it to them? If not, do you say anything to their date?

Your mom is going to be arrested on trumped-up felony charges. She'll never be convicted or imprisoned, but her arrest and mug shot will be major local news. You have the option of taking the blame for her, but you have to agree to complete a full year of community service where you clear dog poop from city streets. What do you choose?

Would you be more willing to push a racist, hateful, foulmouthed, elderly person down the stairs in their wheelchair or post a naked photo of yourself on the Internet for everyone to see?

I mean . . . they kind of had it coming . . .

You're renting out your place on Airbnb to a lovely older couple. If you left one object that you own on their bed that would freak them out the most, what would it be?

What superpower (any superpower you can think of) would you give to your worst enemy?

Would you rather give Hugh Hefner a deep-tissue full-body massage or have sex using Purell hand sanitizer as lubricant?

You're tasked with writing a three-sentence ad in the back of an adult magazine promoting your favorite childhood character. Who is the lucky character and what's the bio you write?

....

Some options to get your started: Kermit the Frog, Barney the Dinosaur, Popeye the Sailor Man.

Two hundred years from now, your name is used as a slur. What does it mean?

Maybe it refers to some annoying personality trait, or the worst thing you've ever done, or some horribly embarrassing public experience. Get creative!

You get to infiltrate the dreams of your worst enemy and direct a feature-length nightmare starring you. What's your 30-second pitch for it?

It's a dream, so there's no budget cap. You're only limited by your imagination. Go hog-wild!

You pull a Pinocchio and, due to your own idiocy, get swallowed whole by an extremely endangered whale species. You find yourself stuck in its belly all alone. There are only two (a male and a female) whales of this kind left on the planet. You have a pocketknife. Do you go down quietly or wipe the species off the map?

Somehow you find out that your best friend and your mother are having an affair. You can only tell one person the news. Do you tell your dad or your best friend's girlfriend?

Either you can never use soap again or you can only use bacon-scented soap for the rest of your life. Which do you choose?

Just remember, everyone loves bacon. Especially hungry stray dogs . . .

Would you rather your roommate catch you stealing cash from them or masturbating to their license photo while wearing a KFC bucket on your head?

Which do you think your roommate would prefer?

You're given the chance to go back in time to when the biblical canon is being finalized and place the script of any comedy or horror film in with the rest of the books. The script will be regarded as a fully legitimate part of the Bible, and its lessons will be followed and incorporated into church law for thousands of years. Which movie do you pick?

Just think about how chillaxed the world would be if 20 percent of the population abided by the lessons of The Dude from *The Big Lebowski*.

Your significant other has to get a full-sized back tattoo of any celebrity. You get to choose who the lucky celebrity will be. Who is your choice and why?

Think about how often someone actually looks at his or her own back. You've got to admit that this is mostly going to be for you.

A line of unisex novelty thongs is being released with your face emblazoned on the crotch. What catchphrase should be included under your picture?

There are no requirements on tone here. Feel free to go with something sexy, funny, ominous, or just plain ridiculous. For me, it's "If you're reading this, I am SO, SO sorry!"

You have to pack an item in your carry-on bag that's legal to own and fly with, but which will totally ruin the day of the TSA agent who finds it in a search. Which item do you pick?

Keep in mind that they do this for a living. They've seen every sex toy under the sun. I'm not quite sure they'd be prepared to deal with my "Daily Turd" photo album, though.

You're a speechwriter for the governor. A few minutes before he is set to deliver memorial remarks at the funeral of a prominent official, you misplace the speech you drafted. All you have time to do is print out lyrics to a song of your choosing. What do you go with?

I might suggest "Tha Crossroads" by Bone Thugs-n-Harmony. It really works for all such occasions.

Your 8-year-old niece has asked for a puppy for her birthday. What nonpuppy animal that fits in a puppy-sized box would you give her for the most disappointing birthday ever?

Note: No one ever said it had to be alive . . .

Your very good friend just started dating a girl who he's head over heels for. His only concern is that she's totally oblivious to the fact that she has a fairly noticeable lady mustache. Being the great friend that you are, you offer to assist. What's your plan to break it to her easy?

It might be worth practicing what you're going to say with someone. Turn to the person to your right and give it a shot.

When you die you can either be cremated and have your ashes baked into a batch of cookies that will be served to your unsuspecting enemies, or you can have your body preserved in the pose of your choice and displayed in the entryway of whichever restaurant or sports venue you prefer. What do you do?

As sad as your loved ones will be to lose you, they'd probably get pretty pumped if they could grab Buffalo wings or see game seven of the World Series every time they visited your "grave."

Pop quiz: You can either go to maximum-security prison for 15 years or fake your own death. If you do the latter, you can't reveal your plan to anyone. All of your friends and family will fully believe that you've died tragically, and you can never see or contact them ever again. Which do you choose?

Is life even worth living if you can't watch your family's annual drunken craziness every Thanksgiving?

Would you rather have both of your legs broken with a baseball bat or share a bathroom with an angry mongoose for at least 3 months?

You must either spike the punch at a middle school dance with LSD or drink a Big Gulp of Mountain Dew straight out of a kangaroo's pouch? Which do you choose?

You wake up tomorrow to find that you've swapped bodies with either Dustin Diamond (Screech from *Saved by the Bell*) or Hillary Clinton. Which would you prefer?

You get to pick any life statistic to be publicly displayed over the head of everyone in the world, such as their current weight, how many people they've slept with, how many pounds of Cheetos they've consumed, etc. What stat do you pick?

Don't forget that the statistic will be displayed over your head as well.

Would you rather cut off your left index finger or have an extremely ugly, but healthy and intelligent, child?

Would you rather spit in the face of a police officer or spend 60 seconds in a field the size of a basketball court with a raging bull?

Whichever you choose you'd better stretch first.

Would you rather retire as a locally respected and loved public high school teacher who inspired hundreds of kids to achieve their dreams and be good people, or a B-list action movie "star" who's appeared in 100-plus direct-to-video films?

I can't imagine life is *that* bad for Dolph Lundgren, the Russian villain from *Rocky IV*, these days . . .

Be real: Which one of the *Golden Girls* would you want to spend a sensual evening with?

Now, now . . . we can't all pick Blanche.

Which famous figure, living or dead, would be the most terrifying to be tickled by?

And which of your family members would you subject to the experience? You always said you'd get grandpa back for forgetting to pick you up from school that one time.

Would you accept $200 in cash every single day for the rest of your life if it meant you had to crap out the bills, clean them, and find places willing to accept your dirty, dirty money?

Would you rather have to hunt and forage to feed your family every day or serve them exclusively free Lean Cuisine dinners for the rest of your lives?

Have you had the Lean Cuisine Chicken Carbonara? To die for.

Take a moment to imagine Charlie Chaplin's mustache and Guy Fieri's hair. Your dad will have to wear one of these styles for the rest of his life. Which do you pick for him?

You're sending a death threat to someone you hate and you want it to be as terrifying as possible. What do you do?

Using crayon in a messy childish scrawl or beautiful calligraphy on the back of a random child's report card would certainly do it for me.

Would you agree to go up 2 full points on the 1–10 attractiveness scale if it meant your breath would smell like buttered popcorn for the rest of your life?

It's not a bad smell, necessarily. But are you going to be able to convince someone to wake up next to it in bed for the rest of their life?

Which one of your exes would be the best romantic match for either your mom or your dad?

Step away from the "Ew!" factor and really think about it. Which pairing would stand the best chance of driving each other crazy?

What's the worst ringtone you can think of to go off during a funeral?

Your child will either be an incurable racist (they didn't learn it from you) or only going to be able to speak German for their entire life. Which would you prefer?

From this moment on, a tiny angel and a tiny devil will appear on your shoulders every time you're about to make a decision between doing the right or wrong thing (just like an old-school cartoon). Which famous figures are going to be your personal angel and devil?

Be careful; are you really going to be able to resist a miniature Kim Kardashian with a pitchfork?

You've been in a pleasant but mediocre relationship with your significant other for 5 years when you suddenly become severely ill. In order to save your life, they give you one of their kidneys. How long do you wait after your surgery until leaving them for the rehab nurse that you've fallen in love with?

Don't forget this isn't just about what they'll think of you, but also how total strangers will see you. Let's be real; there's no way Ellen DeGeneres wouldn't do a story about your partner's generosity.

Santa Claus, the Tooth Fairy, the Easter Bunny, Big Bird, Ronald McDonald, and Mickey Mouse: You have to pick two of these characters to fight to the death in hand-to-hand combat on a children's TV program. Who do you pick?

Who are you putting your money on? I bet Big Bird is a lot scrappier than you'd think . . .

Would you rather have a spouse who exclusively uses cloth adult diapers instead of underwear and the toilet or a spouse who fully reverts to the mentality and intelligence of a baby for 90 minutes each day?

Neither one will be easy to take on vacation with you.

Would you rather be well compensated to give people enemas all day (in a medical setting) or to personally inform the relatives of sick people that their family member only has weeks or months to live?

If a cop offered to let you out of a hefty speeding ticket in exchange for giving a quick kiss to the tip of his boot, would you do it?

Points on your driver's license last 6 years. Your dignity gets renewed what, like, every 3?

For your best friend's wedding gift you have only the option of giving them either a $1,000 gift card to a local car wash or an oil painting of you in a sensual pose. Which are you giving?

Would you rather have every compliment that comes out of your mouth sound acidly sarcastic, or have your voice crack every time you raise your voice to someone?

Look on the bright side. You'll probably raise your texting game in either scenario.

If you agree to have moderate body odor that no amount of bathing or perfume can mask for the rest of your life, then panda bears will thrive as a species. If you decline, they'll go totally extinct within a year. Do you save the pandas or let them fall?

Would you rather wake up to find yourself a conjoined twin with your lifelong crush or your crush's significant other?

Really think about the intimate implications here.

It's your first month at a big new job. Would you rather rip a horrendous nose- and ear-shattering fart during a team meeting with a huge client, or get way too drunk and vomit on the dance floor at the company Christmas party?

Whatever the case, you're definitely walking away with a nickname.

Which have you done more in the last year: Tell your parents you love them or consume an alcoholic beverage?

You're going to be stuck on a desert island for 5 years. For reading material, would you rather have a copy of the Bible or the full 1985–1987 run of *Hustler* magazine?

Would you rather kill, cook, and eat a random gerbil or have your 5-year-old child's beloved pet gerbil (who's also their best friend) die suddenly?

Would you rather get blackout drunk in the middle of your shift as a mall Santa or get blackout drunk in the middle of your shift as a children's barber?

Would you be willing to wipe out every penny of student loan debt in the country if it meant you'd be homeless and living in bitter poverty for the rest of your life?

Just think, actual folk songs would be written in your honor. I mean, you'll probably be put on a postage stamp at some point.

Which would you rather work as, full-time, for an entire year: Full-nude exotic dancer or tenth-grade English teacher in an alternative school for students with severe disciplinary problems? You get paid market rate for either and keep all of your earnings.

I've seen both *Striptease* and *Dangerous Minds*. I liked them both, but *Striptease* was more fun.

An impending meteor impact will wipe out 33 percent of the world's population, but in the post-impact world the survivors will rebuild global society into a peaceful utopia without poverty or greed. You somehow have the ability to avert the collision. Do you do it?

While putting away some clothes in your 16-year-old child's room, would you rather find a batch of steamy letters exchanged with a prison penpal or a baggie of meth and a pipe?

Maybe you shouldn't have let them watch *Orange Is the New Black* after all.

Would you rather have a billion dollars to spend however you wish but die in 15 years or continue your life normally as is?

There's no guarantee you won't die in 15 years anyway . . .

What is the worst form of torture you can devise using only items found in a common first-grade classroom?

You can either die saving a bunch of kids from an orphanage fire and be remembered as a hero, or live to old age and be remembered as the passerby who did nothing to help them. Which do you choose?

You're in severe debt. While at a baseball game you catch a historic record-breaking homerun in the stands. The ball is worth millions at auction, but it was almost caught by a little kid with cancer sitting next to you. You're on the Jumbotron. Do you keep the ball, pay off your loans, and have everyone think you're a Grinch, or do you give it up and be a poor hero?

Either way this moment will be replayed on ESPN pretty much until the end of time.

Which would you rather find on your significant other's cellphone: Nudes of a random person you don't recognize or random nudes of yourself that you don't remember posing for?

You're going to wake up tomorrow as the Disney villain of your choice. Who do you pick?

Remember, Jafar is now a genie and Ursula's anatomy (aside from requiring a saltwater environment) would make it extremely difficult to fit in a car much less drive it.

What childhood memory about your parents, that they don't know you saw or remember, could you most effectively use to silence them in a heated argument?

Think hard. No one can be on the ball for 18 years straight. You most definitely caught them slipping at some point . . .

You hear your roommate pull into the driveway and you run into their bedroom closet, planning on jumping out for a good scare. However, as you see through the crack in the door, they've brought someone over for a little hot 'n heavy action and they waste no time getting into it. Do you reveal yourself immediately and make everything awkward, or do you stay as silent as possible and risk it becoming epically more awkward?

This definitely has the makings of the best Snickers "Not going anywhere for a while?" commercial of all time.

A genie grants you three wishes, but you can't use them to gain anything for yourself or the rest of the world. You can only take things away from specific individuals. What do you take and from whom?

It doesn't have to be a material thing. You could take Donald Trump's money . . . or his sense of self-worth.

You've decided to fake a physical impairment of some kind in order to compete in the Paralympic Games. Which event do you think you could most easily dominate?

Make no mistake—you are a terrible, terrible person.

Would you rather fake a cancer diagnosis and raise $150,000 on GoFundMe for treatment (and be discovered as a fraud a few months later) or meet the person of your dreams but fail to disclose a sexually transmitted disease to them out of fear of their rejection (and have them find out only when they contract it a few months later after you've both said "I love you")?

You can either pick your own food from the garbage every night or cook a gourmet meal for your boss every night and only eat from the leftovers. Which do you choose?

If it makes a difference, you would be supplied with a beautiful kitchen and fine ingredients. You could do some serious *Iron Chef*–level practice.

From now on, every wedding gift you ever buy has to be purchased at either Hot Topic or a porn shop. Which do you choose?

Just think of all the ironic T-shirts and black lipstick you could set newlyweds up with!

Would you rather have "FUCK" or "Tickle Me" tattooed on your forehead?

One is certainly more intimidating. The other is going to get you into much more interesting conversations at parties.

How much money would it take for you to allow an episode of *Jeopardy!* to air where all of the answers are about details of your private life and the contestants are your mom, your best friend, and an ex?

You're deeply in love with your significant other, but you're cheating on them in a meaningless side fling. They find out. Do you feel better if they barely care at all because they've been doing the same thing, or if they're utterly devastated and end your relationship immediately while sobbing uncontrollably?

Your entire extended family (yourself included) is put in a no-holds-barred steel cage match until only one person is left standing. Which relative are you putting your money on to emerge bloody but victorious with the belt?

Grandmas are scrappy . . .

Would you raise the age of consent to 22 years old across the country or make booze and weed legal for anyone over 16?

Suppose the stereotypical versions of Christian Heaven and Hell exist (harps and clouds vs. fire and brimstone) and that everyone ends up in one of them when they die. Would you rather live in a Heaven where you always have to conduct yourself like you're visiting your grandparents on your best behavior or in a Hell where you suffer most of the time but you get a 3-hour break to do whatever each day?

Beginning tomorrow, all real-world person-to-person communication will be governed by the rules of the social network of your choice (for example, in a Snapchat world, all correspondence disappears after being read). Which network's set of rules do you choose for the world? What will be the most annoying thing to adjust to?

Would you rather prank call a nursing home full of lonely seniors hoping to hear from their loved ones or catcall a group of Hells Angels while at a red light?

Shame can last a lifetime. But then again, biker beatings really, really hurt.

You're sitting in a mall food court completely absorbed in your iPhone when you hear a kid laughing. You look up to see a mother give her beaming 4-year-old an ice cream cone as the two of them walk past you. Which would you rather have happen next: You accidentally drop your phone and the screen gets cracked or the kid trips and their ice cream falls on the ground?

You're a high school teacher facing a life crisis and in need of some serious cash. You have the option to either take up prostitution or manufacture crystal meth. You're extremely qualified for whichever one you choose. Which do you pick?

Note to the producers of both *Hung* and *Breaking Bad*: Please don't sue me.

You can either wear braces for the rest of your life (they won't do any damage to your teeth) or everyone you're sexually involved with will have horrible bad breath on Wednesdays, Saturdays, and Mondays. Which one do you choose?

Would you rather have a 5-second make-out session with someone who hasn't brushed their teeth in a year or eat a live spider?

You're being portrayed as an absolute scumbag in a huge Hollywood biopic. Which star both looks enough like you and can bring the perfect amount of scumbagginess (it's a word) to the role?

Would you prefer to be nearsighted to the point of legal blindness or be able to see exactly how and when everyone you meet is going to die?

In your lifetime, which have you done more frequently: Helped someone move or given someone the finger?

Most leases only last a year. Meeting assholes is an everyday occurrence.

You're in a bad financial situation and you need to sell the childhood home you inherited from your parents. If disclosing the fact that the previous family was brutally murdered in the basement (let's assume you're under no legal obligation to divulge this information about that murdered family) meant receiving $30,000 less for the house, would you be honest with prospective buyers?

Would you prefer that your partner cheats on you in one night of passion with their celebrity crush and has an amazing time or that they have drunken St. Patrick's Day dumpster sex with a random person off the street and regret it?

You find out that once, many years ago, your mother had an affair and you're actually not the biological child of the dad who raised you. Obviously this is going to make things a little weird around Father's Day now, but awkwardness aside, which major celebrity would you be most jazzed to have as your new dad?

Follow-up question you probably don't want to think about: Who do you think your mom would be most happy with?

Would you be willing to listen only to Austrian symphony music for the rest of your life if it meant you'd never feel sadness again?

Good luck making your next workout playlist.

What's the most disappointing item that you could give out to trick-or-treaters on Halloween that would actually be useful to a child?

Don't cop out with erasers or other school supplies. Get creative.

Would you rather have your wisdom teeth extracted without anesthesia or have everyone in your family wake up to find that their teeth have been replaced with baby teeth?

You have a secret online dating profile under an alias. Things get weird and you get matched up with both your cousin and your landlord. Who would it be weirder to get an unsolicited nude picture from?

Every pet dog in the world is going to be replaced with an animal of your choice. Your options are sheep, goat, pig, koala, snake, or parrot. Which of these do you choose to have every former dog owner wake up to in the morning?

I'm making no promises that the new animal is really into being someone's pet.

Would you rather have 1 week of extra healthy life for every time you've wanted to kill your loved one or for every time you've hugged a loved one?

Depending on your past, are you okay with the potential for near immortality?

Which cartoon or comic book villain would you let babysit your kids for 4 hours a day?

They might not be the best role models, but there's no way Doctor Doom or Lex Luthor won't teach them some valuable lessons about leadership.

Would you rather have the world rate for alcoholism increase by 5 percent next year or never have a drink again in your life?

Think of all the money you could save if you passed on that weekly bottle of wine.

What's the biggest lie you've ever told in order to get a job?

A horrible and deadly disease is going to be named after you. Based on your temperament and how you treat your own body, what are its top three symptoms?

Mine are definitely a constant low-level hangover, the type of bloating specific to having eaten way too much pizza, and a deep depression whenever reflecting on the cancellation of the TV series *Battlestar Galactica*.

Let's say you find out you're living in the Matrix (a virtual reality world designed to seem real while in actuality your body is really floating in a tub of pink goo that is used to power our ruthless machine overlords). Would you take the blue pill (forget this new knowledge and live on as normal) or the red pill (get freed but face a life of deprivation and constant danger)?

Red pill advantages: Kung fu mastery and standing up for the principles of human freedom. Blue pill advantages: Excellent food, blue skies, not being chased by computer programs that are better at kung fu than you.

For the rest of your life you will be filmed and live-streamed each time you do one of the following activities: Shower, defecate, or have sex. You get to keep any and all proceeds generated from the stream channel. Which of the activities do you pick to share with the world forever?

Would you prefer if your most annoying coworker was fired outright or if they were offered a 20 percent pay bump to clean the bathrooms and serve beverages on demand to everyone in your company?

Either your best friend gets laid off with 2 week's pay or you lose the ability to copy and paste on electronic devices for the rest of your life. Which do you pick?

Think about how much you use copy and paste on a daily basis. There will always be job listings.

Think of the worst way you've ever been dumped and the worst way in which you've dumped someone. Which method would you prefer for your best friend if they were getting dumped tomorrow?

Your third-grader has snuck into your bedroom to grab an item for their classroom show and tell. Which item would you be the least horrified to have them present: A vibrator that they think is a magic wand, a bag of weed that they think is smelly flowers, or a box of condoms they think are balloons?

Which scenario would stress you out more, dating O.J. Simpson or having Casey Anthony babysit your kid?

Would you rather that every moment of your life is live-streamed on the Internet or that everyone within 5 feet of you would be able to read your mind?

You have to send your best friend to work after dosing them with either speed or acid. What do you choose?

Really think about their line of work here. Speed is most likely better for a soccer coach while a librarian would probably fare better on acid.

Human civilization is wiped from the earth and all of our libraries, museums, and monuments crumble into dust. Which literary collection would you decide to use as the building block for a renewed global culture: The books, magazines, and artwork that you own right now, or any one season of *Sesame Street*?

Think long and hard about whether your copy of *The Da Vinci Code*, a sophomore-year biology textbook, and that poster of Vincent van Gogh's *Starry Night* are going to bring more to the table for human advancement than one year of prime Big Bird and Grover banter.

A new nationwide law is put in place for mortuaries: Burial is outlawed and next of kin now need to supply their own containers for the ashes of the deceased. Your most beloved family member just passed away and you're in a bad financial spot. What object that's currently in your kitchen or bathroom would you use to keep the ashes in?

Advice: Do *not* choose a colander.

Would you rather dump someone who treated you like crap via a public Facebook post that airs out all of their dirty laundry or via a skywritten message above their workplace?

Someone has cultivated a strain of marijuana that causes those who use it to exhibit exaggerated versions of your worst personality traits. What's the strain called?

Would you agree to have people see you as stunningly attractive all the time in exchange for being allowed to have sex only a maximum of once every other month?

You've somehow managed to forget that it's the birthday of your best friend in the entire world. You realize this 2 minutes before they arrive at your house to hang out. What item that you currently own can you turn into the most believable "thoughtful" gift that will be happily accepted?

You must either listen to all of your music exclusively on cassette for the rest of your life or your cousin will wake up tomorrow with 50 percent hearing loss in their left ear. They'll never know the cause. Which do you choose?

If you are younger than 25 years of age, take out your phone and Google "cassette tape tangling."

Which is greater: The number of times you've given money to a panhandler on the street or the number of times you've dropped change on the ground and left it there because you didn't feel like bending over?

The truth hurts, don't it?

Would you rather die peacefully but relatively unknown in your sleep in 5 years or become the first person to be struck and killed by a self-driving car in 5 years?

Think about it: Go out in your bed or become the answer to an obscure trivia question?

Would you prefer it if your farts smelled like fresh Cinnabon rolls but were as loud as an air horn or if they smelled bad enough to make people's eyes water but were totally silent and untraceable?

But seriously, have you ever had a Cinnabon? Ah-mah-zing.

Would you be willing to accept a national holiday honoring John Wilkes Booth if it meant you got an extra 3-day weekend every year?

Before you say "Hell no," let's revisit Christopher Columbus's list of accomplishments, shall we?

You've been tasked with choosing the next host for a long-running children's educational TV show, but your pool of candidates is limited to current or former cast members of *Jersey Shore*, *Keeping Up with the Kardashians*, or *The Bachelor/The Bachelorette*. Who do you choose?

Admit it, *Snooki's Story Hour* just sounds like a classic kids show anyway.

Would you choose to wake up to $500 cash under your pillow every morning for the rest of your life if it meant that everyone on the planet right now would have 1 day shaved off of their lives? No one will ever know about this.

Just think of how you could invest that. At the end of the day, what's really greater—the miracle of life or the miracle of compound interest?

You meet someone on a plane and start talking. You hit it off and immediately start dating. After a year of amazing conversation, effortless emotional connection, and insane physical chemistry, you get engaged. The night before the wedding they reveal that every personal detail about themselves that they've told you (age, background, funny anecdotes, their name, etc.) was a complete fabrication. Do you walk away from them completely, or do you walk down the aisle to see if there's still a chance?

You have the choice between receiving a magical monkey's paw that will grant you five wishes, but it will fulfill them in very literal and potentially troubling ways, or a genie in a magic lamp that will give you three wishes, but you'd only get to say the wish once, and the genie only speaks Arabic and is hard of hearing. Which one do you go with?

Aladdin never had to deal with that crap.

You've been given a mystery gift valued at $50,000. You can do whatever you like with it. Huzzah! But there's a catch: You won't know what the gift is until you open it, and you are legally responsible for whatever it is. Do you open it?

Before you say "Yes," think about how you'd explain $50,000 worth of heroin to your mom.

Grab your phone and take a look at the ten most recently played songs. You have to pick one to be both your wedding song and the national anthem. Which do you choose?

From now on your significant other will either lose the ability to sweat (meaning a life of constantly monitoring their temperature and exertion to avoid dangerously overheating) or they will sweat urine. You have to make the choice for them. What do you choose?

Just remember, this affects you both.

Tomorrow every adult in America will wake up to find they've been given either a handgun and a box of ammunition or $5,000 in debt to a major bank. Which would you prefer?

Yeah, of course, undeserved debt is awful, but *everyone* would have a gun. Think about this.

Would you rather be the wealthy author of smutty romance novels or write the next great American novel, but not have it appreciated until after your death?

They say, "love don't pay the rent" . . . but does it?

You've been given the opportunity to go back in time. You can either stop the *Titanic* from sinking or guarantee that your grandfather acquires great wealth and power, which will be passed down through the generations to you. Which do you choose?

Just ask yourself: What would Marty McFly do?

You've successfully started your own cult. Congrats! Your followers worship you and obey you completely. What's the first commandment that all must obey at all times?

Would you rather wake up to find that you have a totally fit, toned, and muscular body but only 50 percent of your current physical strength or that your weight has ballooned significantly, but you have superhuman strength?

If you could steal the skill of any talented and famous individual for yourself, leaving them totally inept in that field, would you do it? For example, you can play ball like Stephen Curry but he'll forget how to dribble, or you can sing like Adele but she wouldn't be able to carry a tune.

If you do go through with it, is it more because the person's so great at what they do or because you can't stand them?

Would you rather have your Internet activity for the rest of your life displayed in real time on a massive screen in Times Square or go without use of the Internet for the rest of your life?

Plus side: If you decided to let it all hang out for millions to see, you could definitely count on some sponsorship opportunities . . .

What would you rather have named in your honor: A small children's reading room in a tiny public library or a wildly successful line of sex toys (on which you receive a small royalty for every sale)?

Would you rather have the power of invisibility, but only when you are naked, or the ability to read the mind of anyone within 10 feet of you, also only while naked?

I'll leave you to work out the practical applications of either.

Would you rather watch only movies that you've already seen before or only be able to communicate with your family in '90s movie quotes?

Never allow yourself to forget how much emotional weight the *Beethoven* comedy franchise carried at its core.

You're giving a major presentation at a work meeting when all of a sudden a text message notification pops up over your slideshow on the big screen. Would you prefer that it be a salacious nude photo or a scheduling confirmation for a job interview with a rival company?

Pick your awkward here . . .

You're on a packed subway car during rush hour when the stranger in front of you turns around and loudly (and falsely) accuses you of either grabbing their ass or trying to pickpocket them. Which would you prefer?

How would you react to either?

You're a doctor who has to confess to a patient that you made a horrible misdiagnosis the week prior. Would you rather have to tell a dying patient that has been very ill for some time that you were wrong when you told them they'd start improving, or tell a healthy patient who's been deeply depressed for a week that you were wrong when you told them they had a month to live?

It's the morning after a pleasant intimate evening you've just shared with someone following a first date. While they're in the shower you jump on their laptop to quickly check the weather. Would you prefer to discover that they've aggressively stalked you by digging through years of your social media profiles (including LinkedIn and your online journal from high school) or that they're sexually attracted to the cast of the animated kids series *My Little Pony*?